JACKIE ROBINSON

BY ANNE SCHRAFF

Development: Kent Publishing Services, Inc.

Design and Production: Signature Design Group, Inc.

SADDLEBACK EDUCATIONAL PUBLISHING

Three Watson

Irvine, CA 92618-2767

Web site: www.sdlback.com

Photo Credits: pages 11, 27, Zuma Press; page 21, HO/AFP/Getty Images; page 35, TSN/Icon SMI

ISBN-13: 978-1-59905-253-3

ISBN-10: 1-59905-253-9

eBook: 978-1-60291-614-2

Printed in China

1 2 3 4 5 6 10 09 08 07

TABLE OF CONTENTS

Before 1947, black baseball players in the United States could not play for Major League Baseball teams. Instead, they had to play in the National Negro Baseball League. The money was far less than major leaguers received. Players in the Negro baseball clubs had to travel in old buses. Often, they could not stay in hotels or eat in restaurants because of their race.

This all changed when the Brooklyn Dodgers decided to bring an African

American player onto the team. Jackie Robinson played for the Kansas City Monarchs, a Negro club. Scouts from the Dodgers noticed his talent. In 1947 Jackie Robinson became the first black baseball player in the major leagues.

On January 31, 1919, Jack Roosevelt Robinson was born near the town of Cairo in southern Georgia. He lived in a farmhouse on a **sharecropper's** rented land. Jack's middle name, Roosevelt, was chosen to honor President Theodore Roosevelt. He showed more concern for African Americans than some earlier presidents.

Jack's mother, Mallie Robinson, was one of fourteen children. She had a sixth grade education. She was the daughter of Wash and Edna McGriff. Both had been born slaves. When Jack was born, Mallie already had three sons and a daughter.

Jack's father, Jerry Robinson, was one of eleven children. He could neither read nor write. He was a farm laborer. Jerry Robinson was a handsome eighteen-year-old when he first met fourteen-year-old Mallie McGriff. They were friends for three years before marrying in 1909.

Mallie and Jerry Robinson were sharecroppers. They worked on a plantation for twelve dollars a month. Their first child, Edgar, was born in 1910. Frank came in 1911, and Mack in 1914. Willa Mae was born in 1916, and their last child, Jack, in 1919.

Jerry Robinson was a restless man. He often left the family for long periods and then returned. But six months after Jack was born, his father left for good.

Mallie Robinson was alone with five children. They ranged in age from six months to eleven years. She was a strong, spirited young woman. She refused to be pushed around by the white plantation owner. As a result, she was **evicted** from the farmhouse. She was left with no means of support.

Mallie Robinson had a half brother in California. He urged her to move there. On May 21, 1920, Mallie and her five children boarded a train for California. Her youngest son, nicknamed Jackie, was a baby. After she bought some food for the journey and paid her fare, Mallie had just three dollars left. She sewed the money into her petticoat.

Mallie stayed with her half brother when she first arrived in Pasadena, California. Then, she rented a shabby three-room apartment. The kitchen sink was a tin tub. Mallie found a job washing and ironing for a white family. While she was at work, his brothers and sisters cared for Jackie.

Willa Mae went to school, but Jackie was too young. Mallie asked the teacher if he could play in the sandbox outside Willa Mae's room. The teacher agreed. Every day, Jackie played in the sandbox until school was out, and his sister took him home.

Later, the family moved to a larger home. The neighborhood was mostly white. Jackie was about eight when a white neighbor girl hurled racial **slurs** at him. Jackie had heard that the worst thing you could call a white person was a "cracker," so that's what he shouted back at the girl.

Her father charged from the house. Soon, he and Jackie were throwing stones at each other. It ended when the man's wife called him inside. Mallie Robinson ignored incidents of **racism**. She was too strong-willed to be scared off.

In 1924 Mallie Robinson bought a nice house at 121 Pepper Street for her family. There were apple, orange, and fig trees in the yard. The Robinsons raised vegetables and many flowers. They also had chickens, rabbits, and turkeys.

Jackie started school at Grover Cleveland Elementary School. His mother strongly believed in religion and education. She encouraged her children in both.

Money was always short at the Robinsons. Jackie wanted to help out. So, he got a paper route. He mowed grass for the neighbors. He also sold hot dogs during ball games at the nearby Rose Bowl.

Jackie was not a scholar. He did not like school. He disliked studying and hard labor. Soon, he joined a group of boys his age called the "Pepper Street Gang." It was a racially mixed group of kids. All came from poor families.

The boys got into minor trouble with the law. They tossed clods of dirt at passing cars. They snatched golf balls from a golf course and sold them back to the golfers. They stole fruit off stands.

Jackie might have gone on to more serious trouble if not for the efforts of two men. One was Carl Anderson, an African American mechanic at a nearby garage. Anderson had long talks with Jackie telling him that the **mischief** he was doing could turn into serious crime. He might go to jail.

Anderson told Jackie how much that would hurt his mother. That was the thing that really hit home with Jackie. He quit the gang because he did not want to bring grief to his mother.

Rev. Karl Downs also changed Jackie's life. He was the young, black pastor of the church where the Robinsons belonged. Downs was deeply involved with youth. He motivated Jackie and other teenagers to do better.

Jackie's older brother, Edgar, had serious learning problems. Jackie and Edgar were not close. But he had a warm relationship with his brother, Frank. Jackie also idolized his brother,

Mack. He was four and a half years older and a fine athlete.

Mack introduced Jackie to sports. Mack was a track star, an outstanding sprinter, who won a place on the 1936 Olympic team. Mack placed second to the Olympic gold medal winner, Jesse Owens, in the 200-meter-dash.

Jackie graduated from Washington Junior High School in 1935. He enrolled in John Muir Technical School. Once a vocational school, Muir was at that time a fully academic school. Jackie sang in the glee club. He was a 135-pound athlete with good hand-to-eye coordination. He won a spot as shortstop on the baseball team, the Muir Terriers. Jackie lettered in baseball, basketball, football, and track.

Although Jackie had friends from all races, he was aware of racism in

Pasadena. The YMCA would not let African Americans use their swimming pool. Blacks had to sit in separate sections of Pasadena movie houses. They were not welcome at soda fountains.

In January 1937, eighteen-year-old Jackie Robinson enrolled at Pasadena Junior College. He played baseball, football, and tennis. Jackie's brother, Frank, was attending the University of California at Los Angeles. He convinced Jackie to join him there. In the winter of 1939, Jackie drove his 1931 Plymouth to UCLA. He began studying hard. He continued to **excel** at sports.

Soon after he arrived at UCLA, Jackie suffered a painful loss. Frank, his beloved brother, was killed in a motorcycle accident. Grief stricken, Jackie found comfort by throwing himself into sports.

While at UCLA, Jackie met a nursing school freshman, Rachel Annetta Isum. They began dating. Soon, Jackie Robinson decided to quit college. He wanted to get a job so he could help his mother with money. He also wanted to plan his future with Rachel. He looked for a job working in sports with youth.

CHAPTER 3

Jackie Robinson got a job with the National Youth Administration. It was a government program to help youth. He worked at a camp in Atascadero, California. The job ended quickly when the facility was turned into an army camp. Robinson then thought about a career in professional sports, playing baseball or basketball.

At the time, no Major League Baseball clubs hired black players. If you were black and wanted to play baseball, you could only play for the Negro League for poor pay and difficult working conditions.

Robinson decided to get a job in construction. Later, he worked for Lockheed Aircraft. He was making enough money to help his mother. But he was still looking for a career.

The United States was at war with Germany, Japan, and Italy after the December 1941 bombing of Pearl Harbor. The military **draft** was calling on millions of young American men to serve. On March 23, 1942, Jackie Robinson was drafted into the United States Army. He was sent to Fort Riley, Kansas, for his basic training.

Jackie Robinson was designated an expert **marksman**. He was a applied to

Jackie Robinson was drafted into the United States Army

army Officer Candidate School. But was turned down. He was given the job of caring for the horses in the army stable. Robinson tried to join the army baseball team, but only white soldiers were accepted.

When he applied again for Officer Candidate School, he was approved. He received his 2nd Lieutenant's gold bars in January, 1943. He was now engaged to be married to Rachel Isum. She studied at the San Francisco School of Nursing.

Robinson was sent to Camp Hood, Texas. He joined the 761st Tank Battalion. He was scheduled to go overseas when an ankle injury delayed him.

While riding home from a medical examination on a bus, Robinson sat beside a white female officer. They began talking. The bus driver noticed this and stopped the bus. He told Robinson that it was wrong for a black officer to sit beside a white officer. Both Robinson and the white officer ignored the bus driver, and military police were called.

Jackie Robinson was called in to headquarters. He was questioned about the incident. Robinson felt some of the questions were racist and objectionable. He did not respond to them.

Robinson was then **court martialed** on charges that he was disrespectful to an officer and that he disobeyed orders. The matter came to trial. Robinson was found innocent of all charges. But his military career was over. He received an honorable discharge from the army in November 1944.

Now twenty-six and a **civilian** again,

Robinson once more considered a career in sports. He was invited to play for the Kansas City Monarchs in the Negro National League. He reported to Houston for training. He played shortstop. Robinson earned $400 a month.

The schedule for the Negro leagues was hectic. The teams rode buses to their games. Players often found themselves in cities where there were no hotels or restaurants for African Americans. The usual routine was to sleep on the bus. Players would grab their dinners served in greasy bags from the back doors of restaurants.

Black people could not sit in most restaurants and eat with white patrons. They could only sit down in restaurants in large cities where they could find them in black neighborhoods. Travel for the black baseball players was a rough, **humiliating** experience.

There were fine black baseball players like LeRoy "Satchel" Paige and catcher Josh Gibson. They were barred from the major leagues just because of their color. In boxing, Joe Louis held the heavyweight title longer than any man. He was known as the "Brown Bomber." It seemed that time had come for baseball to tear down the color barrier.

Jackie Robinson wearing a Kansas City Monarchs uniform.

CHAPTER 4

Branch Rickey was the coach for Ohio Wesleyan University when he went to South Bend, Indiana, for a football game. One of Rickey's players was black. His name was Charley Thomas.

The Ohio Wesleyan team went to a hotel in South Bend. They were told Thomas was not welcome. Rickey said that if the hotel refused Thomas, then none of the team members would stay there. The hotel would not change its rule.

Finally, they reached a compromise. A cot was brought into Rickey's room. Thomas was told he could sleep there. Thomas felt so humiliated that he could not sleep. He spent the night sitting on the cot weeping.

Branch Rickey never forgot that night. Thirty-five years later, Rickey was head of the Brooklyn Dodgers baseball team. He recalled the humiliation of Charley Thomas and decided he would tear down the color line in baseball. Rickey was determined to hire a black player for the Dodgers.

Rickey's plan was called "the Noble Experiment." Many in Major League Baseball believed it would not work. But Rickey thought it was the right thing to do.

He knew that black players would help win games. Rickey's scouts began watching Negro League games looking for talent. They wanted to find that perfect black baseball player to break into the all-white major leagues.

By August 1945, Jackie Robinson was tired of playing with the Monarchs. He was about ready to give up his dream of a baseball career. He wanted to marry Rachel Isum and get a job as a high school coach in Los Angeles. Rachel could work as a nurse, and they could get on with life.

But Rickey's scouts spotted Robinson. They were impressed. On August 24, they contacted him and said Branch Rickey wanted to see him. Robinson believed he was being considered for the Brooklyn Brown Dodgers, a Negro team.

When Robinson walked into Rickey's office, he was told he was a candidate for the Brooklyn Dodgers. Robinson was excited and speechless. But Branch Rickey made it clear that he was not just looking for a fine black baseball player. He was looking for a very unusual man. Robinson would need the courage to withstand terrible abuse and pressure without striking back.

Rickey told Robinson that some of the umpires, the fans, owners, and other players would be against him. Rickey said Robinson would have to be a gentleman under all conditions. He would have to stand and take whatever came his way.

Robinson had always stood up for himself. When he was the victim of racial abuse, he struck back. If he were to accept Rickey's offer, he could not do that anymore.

Rickey told Robinson that it was not only a matter of whether he could run, throw, and hit. He also needed to take psychological and even physical abuse. Rickey went so far as to dramatize the ugly situations that might occur. Rickey played the role of a rude hotel clerk denying Robinson a room. He portrayed a bigoted waiter refusing Robinson a table. Rickey played the role of a foul-mouthed fan screaming racial insults from the stands. He even swung a fist at Robinson's head.

Jackie Robinson listened to all the warnings. He told Rickey he could take whatever was thrown at him. What's more, he could help the Brooklyn Dodgers win a **pennant**. Robinson said he would do it for all black youth, for his mother, for Rachel and himself, and for Branch Rickey who was taking a very big chance. Rickey was defying decades of racism in the major leagues.

Robinson had spent two hours with Rickey. He left his office with a player's contract and a book about the life of Christ with passages on turning the other cheek when attacked underlined by Rickey. Robinson would be paid a $3,500 signing bonus and a salary of $600 a month.

For Jackie Robinson and Major League Baseball, a new day had dawned.

Jackie Robinson warming up before a Brooklyn Dodgers game.

On February 10, 1946, Jackie Robinson married Rachel Isum in the Independent Church of Christ. It was the largest black church in Los Angeles. Rev. Karl Downs flew in to perform the ceremony. Some members of the old Pepper Street Gang attended the wedding. Then, Rachel and Jackie Robinson headed for spring training. Baseball camp began in March 1946 in Daytona Beach, Florida.

Like all new players, Robinson would begin playing for the Dodger farm team, the Montreal Royals. It was clear from the start that racism would be a problem for the Robinsons in Florida. The rest of the team stayed in a local hotel. The Robinsons lived at the home of a black family in town.

The Montreal Royals moved their camp to Sanford, Florida. Robinson, and one other black player, John Wright, joined 200 white players for practice. Most of the white players were Southerners.

They were not hostile to Robinson and Wright, but they weren't friendly either. Rachel Robinson was one of the few wives there most of the time. She gave her husband a lot of moral support.

Early in some **exhibition games**, trouble surfaced. The games had to be cancelled since the Royals had black players. Cities like Jacksonville, Florida,

Savannah, Georgia, and Richmond, Virginia had laws against blacks and whites playing games together.

The regular season opened in Jersey City, New Jersey, on April 18, 1946, in Roosevelt Stadium. Twenty-five thousand people came to see the Jersey City Giants play the Montreal Royals. Many black fans appeared for the history-making game.

It was Jackie Robinson's **debut** and the fans did not know what to expect. When Robinson delivered his first home run, the fans went wild, screaming, stamping their feet, and laughing.

Robinson hit safely four times, including the home run. He stole second base twice. The fans roared. They loved the reckless courage of the young black man.

For decades, many people falsely believed that black athletes were basically inferior to whites. In this first game, Robinson demolished the stereotype. He was a nervy, thrilling player. Montreal won 14 to 1. Happy fans mobbed the team as they left the field. Both black and white, young and old cheered Robinson.

After the great triumph in Jersey City, the cold hard facts of life came to light in Baltimore, Maryland. Rachel Robinson sat in the stands as usual. Two white men behind her began making ugly racial slurs against her husband. Insults flew from all over the stands directed against Robinson. Robinson kept his promise to Branch Rickey. He remained calm and played well.

The Robinsons moved to Montreal, Canada, while Jackie played with the Royals. They rented a house in a white neighborhood. All the neighbors were French, and although they spoke no English, they were warm and friendly. Rachel charmed the Canadian women with her poise and charm.

For the Robinsons, living in Montreal was a joy. They found none of the racism that existed in parts of the United States. Robinson was dubbed the "colored comet" in Montreal, as he maintained a .356 batting average.

During one game against Syracuse, a rival player threw a black cat into the dugout. The white player jeered, "Here's your cousin." Robinson scored in the game and told his abuser that since he was playing so well, his "cousin" must be proud.

Robinson coped with the racial insults and abuse with tact and good humor. But keeping all his frustration inside was hard. He often couldn't sleep or eat. The fans marveled at Robinson's self control. *Newsweek* called him a big league ballplayer and a gentleman.

When the Montreal Royals went to play the Jersey City Giants in Jacksonville, Florida, they found the ballpark locked. It was because of Robinson's presence on the team. But, Robinson's first year in the big leagues was a triumph. He was the top batter in the league.

In the final game of the season, he won the championship for Montreal. Robinson made his way through the crowds of adoring fans after the game. Women kissed him. Children crowded around him. He was **hoisted** to the shoulders of the fans.

On November 18, 1946, Rachel Robinson gave birth to the couple's first child, Jack Junior, at Good Samaritan Hospital in Los Angeles. On April 10, 1947, Branch Rickey called Robinson to tell him he was now a member of the Brooklyn Dodgers.

Jackie Robinson was given the number 42. He earned a salary of $5,000 a year. He became a first baseman. Robinson's excitement dimmed when some members of the Dodger team signed a petition saying they would not play on the same team with a black man.

It hurt even more that these players were on a Northern team, though they were all Southerners. Branch Rickey told the protesting players that if they did not want to play with Robinson they could all quit. Robinson was on the team to stay.

Jackie Robinson signs a contract to become the first black player in Major League Baseball. Branch Rickey, General Manager of the Dodgers, sits by his side.

Early in the season, the Brooklyn Dodgers **played** the Philadelphia Phillies in Ebbets Field. The southern-born manager of the Phillies encouraged his players to attack Robinson verbally. Vile racist taunts rose from the Philly dugout when Robinson appeared.

The taunts were so **relentless** that later Robinson described that day as one of the worst of his life. He was not sure if he could take it. He wanted to punch his abusers in their faces and then walk off the field and out of baseball.

After seven scoreless innings, Robinson had the winning run. The Philly players increased their abuse. Suddenly, Robinson's fellow Dodgers chimed in on his side. They yelled at the Philly players and called them yellow cowards. Dodger shortstop Pee Wee Reese, who was from Kentucky, stood out as a Robinson friend and ally.

Jackie and Rachel Robinson loved the Brooklyn fans. They especially loved the elderly ladies who came faithfully to every game. They always cheered for Robinson.

In June 1947 Robinson helped lift the Dodgers to first place. They won the pennant. September 22, 1947, was named Jackie Robinson Day in Ebbets Field. Robinson won the Rookie of the Year award.

He made the September 22 cover of *Time* magazine. He led the Dodgers in runs scored (125), singles bunt hits (14), total bases and bases stolen (28), and home runs (12). His season batting average was .297.

In the World Series against the New York Yankees, Robinson played well, but the Yankees won. In the 1947 season, Jackie Robinson had proved that a black athlete could be outstanding. He changed the negative image of the young black male. He was not only a great athlete, but he showed courage. He showed physical power and dignity in the face of terrible verbal abuse.

In a 1947 contest, Jackie Robinson was named the second most admired man in America He was surpassed in popularity only by the singer Bing Crosby. **Endorsements** for many products gave Robinson a good second income.

Jackie Robinson credited his wife for keeping him focused and calm during the first season. When many young athletes allow fame to go to their heads, Robinson kept his principles. He refused alcohol and tobacco. When attractive girls approached him, he told them he had vowed to be faithful all his life to his wife, Rachel.

The 1948 season was average for Robinson. He was moved to second base. Robinson had become a much-admired role model for young Americans, especially blacks.

In 1949 he was caught up in a political **controversy**. Another prominent black American, singer Paul Robeson, stated that if the United States went to war against the Soviet

Union, young American blacks would refuse to serve. This shocked many people.

People wanted a patriotic young black man to **refute** this idea. They turned to Jackie Robinson. He was asked to come to Washington and address the House Un-American Activities Committee. It was investigating communist, pro-Soviet activity in the United States. This committee believed that Robeson was pro-communist and that was why he made the shocking statement.

Jackie Robinson respected Paul Robeson as a man who had fought long and hard against racial discrimination in the United States. Robinson could understand how frustrated Robeson was. Thousands of black soldiers served in the U.S. Army during World War II. Yet, they still were not treated with equality.

Robinson understood why Robeson made that comment. But he did not agree with it. He went to Washington and told the committee that Robeson was not speaking for all blacks. Robinson said he **cherished** America. He said he would continue to help create a more just society.

In 1949 Jackie Robinson again helped the Brooklyn Dodgers win the National League pennant. Robinson was named the most valuable player. The Dodgers however, lost the World Series to the New York Yankees. Robinson signed a new contract with the Dodgers. Daughter Sharon was born on January 13, 1950.

CHAPTER 7

In 1950 the Robinsons bought their own home in the St. Albans section of Long Island. It was primarily a white neighborhood. A motion picture—*The Jackie Robinson Story*—was made, starring Robinson. He liked the movie, but later on believed it was made too quickly and was not as well done as it could have been.

During the 1950 spring training season, Jackie Robinson Junior was three-years-old. He became a favorite at camp. He seemed to be enjoying himself. But the popping cameras and attention sometimes frightened him. Even at this young age, the boy seemed extremely sensitive.

Spring training was in Vero Beach, Florida. A separate facility for blacks was the rule. The wives of white players went to one beauty shop. It did not serve blacks.

One day, Rachel Robinson was on her way to the black beauty salon with her son. She hailed a cab. She was told black fares were not welcome. She waited a long time for the black cab. Rachel Robinson was angry and upset. She felt her little boy noticed her mood.

In 1950 Branch Rickey, Jackie Robinson's biggest supporter, left the Dodgers. Walter O'Malley replaced him. Robinson felt that O'Malley did not like him.

Still, 1950 was a good year for Robinson. He was awarded the George Washington Carver Institute's Gold Medal for contributions to his race. The Dodgers were tied with the Philadelphia Phillies for the National League pennant and eventually lost.

In 1951 the Dodgers lost the pennant to the New York Giants. In May 1952 the Robinson's third child, David, was born. The Brooklyn Dodgers won the pennant, but again lost the World Series to the New York Yankees.

In 1953 Jackie Robinson was a guest on the television show *Youth Wants to Know*. He said, in response to a question, that he thought the New York Yankees discriminated against blacks. At the time, they were the only Major League Baseball club without a single black player. Robinson's comment brought a storm of angry letters. He was not supposed to say anything **controversial**.

The Robinsons moved to Stamford, Connecticut, in 1953. The Brooklyn Dodgers won the National League pennant with Robinson's help in 1952 and 1953, losing both times in the World Series to the New York Yankees.

Jackie Robinson longed for the Dodgers to win a World Series. In 1955 it happened. It was once again the Brooklyn Dodgers against the New York Yankees. The Dodgers won the final game. It was one of the great thrills of Robinson's life.

The Robinsons enrolled their son, Jackie, in an all white school in Connecticut. They believed he would get the best education there. But the boy was the only black student in the school.

He did poorly. Later, the Robinsons regretted sending him to that school. He had felt like an outsider.

The 1956 baseball season was Robinson's last. He had helped the Dodgers win their first World Series. Now, at 37, he was ready to start a new career. Robinson spent some time playing golf. He **pondered** several business offers.

At that time, black baseball players who retired did not have opportunities in baseball management. So, Robinson became a manager for the food company, Chock Full O'Nuts. He also spent a lot of time doing volunteer work. He raised money for the National Association for the Advancement of Colored People (NAACP).

In 1960 Jackie Robinson became active in politics. Most American blacks supported Democrat John F. Kennedy for president. But Robinson supported

Vice President Richard Nixon, a Republican. When Kennedy became president, Robinson grew to respect him and his brother, Attorney General Robert Kennedy, for their support of civil rights causes.

By 1960, the Robinsons were very worried about their 14-year-old son, Jackie. He was having serious trouble in school. His sister Sharon and brother David were happy and doing well, but Jackie Junior was quiet and withdrawn.

He did not take part in activities the other children enjoyed, such as horseback riding. He did poorly in sports. He failed at baseball. The Robinsons sent the boy to a **psychologist**. Then they sent him to a private boarding school. They hoped this would help him outgrow his problems.

On July 23, 1962 in Cooperstown, New York, 43-year-old Jackie Robinson won baseball's highest honor. He was inducted into the National Baseball Hall of Fame. In his acceptance speech, he thanked his mother, his wife, and Branch Rickey for making this crowning achievement possible.

Jackie Robinson became more active in civil rights work. He became a close friend of Dr. Martin Luther King Jr. He also wrote an opinion column for the *Amsterdam News*.

Rachel Robinson achieved her long time dream of getting a masters degree in psychiatric nursing. She became the Director of Nursing at the New Haven State Mental Health Center.

In the early 1960s, health problems began to sap Jackie Robinson's strength. A knee operation led to blood poisoning. Robinson had to use a cane to walk. His hair turned prematurely gray, and he looked much older than he was.

In 1964 he left his job at Chock Full O'Nuts. He campaigned for New York Governor Nelson Rockefeller to become the Republican candidate for president. Robinson was disappointed when Rockefeller failed to get the nomination.

Robinson suffered from diabetes. It affected his eyes, legs, and heart. But he continued to be active. In 1964 he helped launch the Freedom National Bank, a Harlem bank that served black business people. Robinson also spoke around the country on such topics as poverty, urban development, and youth problems. In March 1965 he joined ABC-TV Sports as a commentator.

All during this time, Jackie Jr's problems **mounted**. He failed boarding school and briefly ran away to California with a friend. The police brought him home. Jackie Robinson's relationship with his son grew more troubled. They had a hard time speaking to one another.

Jackie Jr. enlisted in the United States Army at the time the Vietnam War was raging. Jackie Jr. took his basic training at Fort Riley as his father had done. In June 1965 Jackie Jr. was sent to

Vietnam. It was a painful time of worry for his parents. Many young Americans were getting killed and wounded in Vietnam.

In November Jackie Jr. and his unit took part in a fierce firefight with the enemy. The soldier at either side of Jackie Jr. was killed in the battle. Jackie Jr. was wounded. During the battle, he had dragged a wounded comrade to safety. Jackie Jr. was awarded the Purple Heart.

In December Robinson's mentor and friend, Branch Rickey, died. Robinson grieved as a son would for a father. Robinson also helped Gov. Nelson Rockefeller make a successful run for another term as New York's governor.

The Robinsons welcomed their son, Jackie Jr., back from Vietnam in 1966.

But, like many Vietnam veterans, he was confused and bewildered. On March 4, 1968, Jackie Jr. was arrested for possession of marijuana and heroin. He was taken to Stamford jail. His parents were devastated. The young man had been unemployed and aimless since returning from Vietnam. Now, he was in serious trouble.

The Robinsons checked their son into Yale-New Haven Hospital where Rachel Robinson worked in the detoxification unit. When Jackie Jr.'s case came to court, he was given a choice. He could enroll in a strict rehabilitation program or go to jail.

The young man had been seriously addicted in Vietnam to cocaine and amphetamines. Jackie Jr. chose rehabilitation. He became a resident at Daytop rehabilitation program in

Seymour, Connecticut. A tough program with hard discipline, it had a staff made up of former drug addicts. The Robinsons supported their son. They visited him often.

During the 1968 election, Jackie Robinson again hoped Nelson Rockefeller would win the Republican nomination. But it went to Richard Nixon. 1968 was a tragic year. It brought the death of Robinson's mother, Mallie. Then came the assassinations of Dr. Martin Luther King Jr. and Robert F. Kennedy, whom Robinson had come to admire.

Robinson suffered a mild heart attack, but he faced the future with hope. Son David and daughter Sharon were doing well. Jackie Jr. seemed to be making excellent progress at Daytop.

CHAPTER 9

In 1970 the Robinsons held a picnic for fifty members of Daytop. They were so grateful for what Daytop had done for their son. After years of estrangement, Jackie Jr. reached out and embraced his father. Now an Assistant Regional Director at Daytop, Jackie Jr. appeared with his father to make motivational speeches and deliver an anti-drug message.

Although he could still help with projects such as Rev. Jesse Jackson's Operation Breadbasket, Jackie had grown very frail. Rachel Robinson took a leave of absence from her job to care for him.

Robinson was always tired and his legs and feet throbbed in pain. He suffered some mild strokes. He lost his sense of balance and some feeling in his left side. The blood vessels in his eyes ruptured. His retina was damaged, and he faced blindness.

In February 1970 the Robinsons celebrated their 25th wedding anniversary. But the doctors found Robinson was suffering from high blood pressure and serious blockage of his arteries.

On June 17, 1971, the Robinsons suffered the greatest tragedy of their lives. 24-year-old Jackie Jr. was driving on Merritt Parkway when he lost control of his car. The car hurtled into a guard rail. The young man's neck was broken, and he died.

When the Robinsons heard the news, they were both crushed. It was all the more painful because Jackie Jr. seemed finally to have overcome his demons. He was a well-respected, effective leader at Daytop. He appeared to have found his niche in life. Jackie Robinson Jr. was buried at Antioch Baptist Church. Many he had helped grieved with his family.

Jackie Robinson picked up the pieces of his life. He continued to carry out his charitable activities. Son David was attending Stanford University in California. Daughter Sharon, after a brief unhappy marriage, was now happily married to a man the Robinsons liked.

Because of his failing sight, Robinson could no longer drive a car. On October 23, 1972, he asked his driver to take him on his usual rounds. Though limping, Robinson delivered meat and canned goods to the poor. He was volunteering with an outreach program from Nazarene Baptist Church.

The next day at 6:26 a.m., Robinson collapsed at his home. Rachel called for help and an ambulance took him to Stamford Hospital. Jackie Robinson was pronounced dead at the age of 53.

C H A P T E R 10

On October 27, between 1 and 9 p.m. Jackie Robinson's body lay in state at a Harlem funeral home. There was a viewing at the Riverside Church as well. The family asked that donations be made to the Daytop program that had done so much for Jackie Robinson Jr.

The funeral was held at noon in Riverside Church on October 29, 1872. Twenty-five hundred mourners came to pay their respects. They included many famous civil rights leaders, Governor

Nelson Rockefeller, and many from the sports world. They also included ordinary people from Daytop, and black fans who could recall the thrill when they first saw a splendid young African American athlete play in the major leagues.

Reverend Jesse Jackson delivered the eulogy for Robinson. Six former athletes carried Robinson's silver and blue coffin. It was covered with red roses. One of the athletes was basketball star Bill Russell from the Boston Celtics.

The other five were former Brooklyn Dodgers who played with Robinson, including his close friend from the early days, Pee Wee Reese. The funeral **cortege** extended for several blocks. Jackie Robinson was taken to Cypress Hills Cemetery and buried near where his son had been laid to rest only a year earlier.

After Jackie Robinson's death, Rachel Robinson established the Jackie Robinson Foundation for college scholarships. Sharon Robinson became a nurse and then a professor at Yale University School of Nursing. David Robinson emigrated to Tanzania to form a cooperative farm. His mother often visited him there.

On March 26, 1984, Jackie Robinson was posthumously awarded the Medal of Freedom, the nation's highest civilian honor. (A posthumous award is one given to a person after his or her death.) In 1996, a bill approved by both houses of Congress authorized the minting of silver and gold coins to commemorate the fiftieth anniversary of Robinson's entry into baseball's major leagues. On April 15, 1997, the number 42 was retired from all Major League Baseball for all time to come.

Jackie Robinson had a career batting average of .311. During the ten years he played for the Brooklyn Dodgers, he helped them win six National League pennants and, in 1955, a World Series.

Impressive as his athletic achievements were, what Jackie Robinson accomplished as a man was far more important. At a time when black players were **banned** from Major League Baseball, he had the courage and dignity to be the first to endure the withering barrage of racism and rejection without responding in kind.

He was a trailblazer, opening the way for so many other black baseball players. Jackie Robinson played baseball, often under terrible pressure, and he proved he was not only a great athlete but also a gentleman. He became a hero to all Americans.

BIBLIOGRAPHY

Rampersad, Arnold. *Jackie Robinson, A Biography.* New York: Alfred A. Knopf, 1997.

Robinson, Jackie. *I Never Had It Made.* New Jersey: Ecco Press, 1995.

GLOSSARY

banned: barred, forbidden

boarding school: a school providing living accommodations for its students

cherished: appreciated, respected, esteemed

civilian: a person who is not a member of the armed forces

controversial: contentious, divisive

controversy: argument, disagreement

cortege: parade for a funeral

court martialed: tried in a military court

debut: first appearance, introduction

draft: conscription, the enforced selection of people to join the military

endorsements: payment for serving as a spokesperson for a product or company

evicted: dispossessed, ejected, forced out

excel: do extremely well, shine, stand out

exhibition games: pre-season games or other games whose results are not included in statistics used to determine rankings

hoisted: lifted

humiliating: demeaning, degrading, embarrassing

marksman: sharpshooter

mischief: trouble

mounted: increased, worsened, piled up

pennant: league championship

pondered: thought about

psychologist: a person trained to help others with mental or behavioral health problems

racism: discrimination, intolerance, bigotry

refute: disprove, contest, counter

relentless: unceasing

sharecroppers: people who farmed land that was owned by a landlord with whom they shared the crops and their proceeds

slurs: insults, affronts

INDEX